Teach Your Granny: Project Management

An Introduction to the Basics of Project Management

Andrew Ward

Table of Contents:

Foreword

Welcome to "Teach Your Granny Project Management," a practical guide designed to make project management accessible and straightforward. Whether you're an experienced professional or new to project management, this book provides the essential tools and knowledge you need to succeed.

My journey in project management began with many challenges and learning experiences. Over time, I discovered that effective project management is rooted in a few fundamental principles and practical strategies that anyone can master.

This book simplifies these principles into easy-to-understand chapters, filled with practical advice and real-world examples. The aim is to demystify project management and offer a clear roadmap for planning, executing, and closing projects.

Project management is not just for large corporations. The techniques discussed here are applicable to projects of all sizes, whether you're planning a family event or leading a team at work.

I hope "Teach Your Granny Project Management" serves as a valuable resource in your project management journey. Let's embark on this path together, turning visions into reality with confidence and success.

Chapter 1: Understanding Project Management

Project management is a critical skill that can be applied to various aspects of life, from organizing a family reunion to launching a new product at work. At its core, project management is about planning, organizing, and managing resources to achieve specific goals. In this chapter, we will explore what project management entails, the role of a project manager, key concepts and terminology, and the stages of the project lifecycle.

What is a Project?

A project is a temporary endeavour undertaken to create a unique product, service, or result. Unlike routine operations, which are ongoing and repetitive, projects have a defined beginning and end. They are designed to accomplish specific objectives within a set timeframe and budget. Projects can vary in size and complexity, from small personal tasks to large organizational initiatives.

Projects can be as simple as planning a birthday party or as complex as constructing a skyscraper. Regardless of their size or scope, all projects share common characteristics:

- **Unique Objectives**: Each project has specific goals that set it apart from routine operations. For example, launching a new product involves different tasks and outcomes than the day-to-day running of a business.
- **Temporary Nature**: Projects have a clear start and finish. They are temporary efforts designed to achieve a particular goal and are not meant to be permanent.

- **Defined Deliverables**: Projects aim to produce specific outputs or deliverables, whether it's a new software application, a marketing campaign, or an event.
- **Resource Constraints**: Projects are typically bound by limited resources, including time, money, and personnel. Effective project management involves making the best use of these resources.

Examples of Projects:

- **Organizing a Wedding**: This involves numerous tasks such as selecting a venue, sending out invitations, planning the ceremony and reception, and coordinating with vendors.
- **Developing a New Software Application**: This project includes defining requirements, designing the application, coding, testing, and deploying the software.
- **Building a New House**: This complex project involves architectural design, obtaining permits, construction, and interior finishing.
- **Planning a Marketing Campaign**: This includes market research, creating promotional materials, launching the campaign, and measuring its effectiveness.
- **Launching a New Business**: This involves creating a business plan, securing funding, setting up operations, and marketing the new venture.

The Role of a Project Manager

A project manager is responsible for leading a project from inception to completion. This role involves coordinating various tasks, managing team members, and ensuring that the project stays on track to meet its goals. The project manager acts as the central point of contact and decision-maker, balancing the needs of stakeholders, the team, and the project itself.

The role of a project manager can be demanding, requiring a combination of leadership, communication, and organizational skills. Successful project managers are adept at handling multiple tasks simultaneously, solving problems, and keeping the team motivated.

Key Responsibilities of a Project Manager:

- **Defining Project Objectives and Scope**: The project manager works with stakeholders to establish clear goals and boundaries for the project. This involves understanding the desired outcomes, setting realistic expectations, and documenting the project scope.
- **Developing Detailed Project Plans**: A comprehensive project plan outlines the tasks, timelines, resources, and milestones required to complete the project. The project manager creates this plan and adjusts it as needed throughout the project lifecycle.
- **Assigning Tasks and Responsibilities**: Effective delegation is crucial in project management. The project manager assigns tasks to team members based on their skills and availability, ensuring that everyone knows their roles and responsibilities.
- **Managing Resources and Budgets**: The project manager is responsible for allocating resources efficiently, managing the project budget, and ensuring that expenditures stay within approved limits.
- **Monitoring Progress and Making Adjustments**: Regularly tracking the project's progress helps identify potential issues early. The project manager monitors key performance indicators (KPIs), manages risks, and makes necessary adjustments to keep the project on track.
- **Communicating with Stakeholders and Team Members**: Clear and consistent communication is vital for project

success. The project manager provides updates, gathers feedback, and addresses concerns from stakeholders and team members.

- **Ensuring the Project Meets its Goals and Deadlines**: Ultimately, the project manager's job is to ensure that the project achieves its objectives on time and within budget. This involves continuous oversight and problem-solving to overcome any obstacles.

Key Concepts and Terminology

Understanding the basic concepts and terminology of project management is essential for anyone involved in a project. Here are some key terms you should know:

- **Scope**: The scope of a project defines its boundaries, including what will be done and what will not be done. It sets the expectations for deliverables and outcomes. A well-defined scope helps prevent scope creep, which is the tendency for project requirements to expand beyond the initial objectives.
- **Stakeholders**: Stakeholders are individuals or groups who have an interest in the outcome of the project. This can include clients, team members, managers, and other parties affected by the project. Identifying and managing stakeholder expectations is critical to project success.
- **Deliverables**: Deliverables are tangible or intangible outputs produced as a result of the project. These can include reports, products, services, or any other results agreed upon. Each deliverable should be clearly defined, measurable, and tied to the project objectives.
- **Milestones**: Milestones are significant points or events in the project timeline. They help track progress and indicate when key phases or tasks are completed. Milestones serve

as checkpoints to assess the project's status and make necessary adjustments.

- **Budget**: The budget is the total amount of money allocated for the project. It includes all costs associated with completing the project, such as labour, materials, and overhead. Effective budget management ensures that the project stays financially viable.
- **Risk**: Risk refers to potential events or conditions that could negatively impact the project. Effective risk management involves identifying, assessing, and mitigating these risks. Risks can be related to technical challenges, resource constraints, or external factors such as market conditions.
- **Work Breakdown Structure (WBS)**: A WBS is a hierarchical decomposition of the total scope of work to be carried out by the project team. It breaks down the project into smaller, manageable components, making it easier to plan, execute, and control.
- **Gantt Chart**: A Gantt chart is a visual representation of the project schedule. It displays tasks along a timeline, showing their start and end dates, duration, and dependencies. Gantt charts are useful for tracking progress and ensuring that tasks are completed on time.
- **Critical Path**: The critical path is the longest sequence of tasks in a project that must be completed on time for the project to meet its deadline. Identifying the critical path helps project managers focus on the most important tasks and manage dependencies effectively.

The Project Lifecycle

The project lifecycle is the series of phases that a project goes through from initiation to completion. Understanding these phases helps in planning and managing a project effectively. The project lifecycle typically includes five stages:

1. **Initiation**:
   - This phase involves defining the project, identifying its purpose, and determining its feasibility. Key activities include developing a project charter, identifying stakeholders, and setting initial objectives. The project charter is a formal document that outlines the project's objectives, scope, stakeholders, and key deliverables. It serves as a reference point throughout the project lifecycle.

2. **Planning**:
   - Planning is critical to the success of any project. During this phase, detailed plans are developed to outline how the project will be executed, monitored, and controlled. Key activities include creating a project plan, developing a schedule, budgeting, and risk management planning. The project plan is a comprehensive document that includes the project scope, objectives, deliverables, timeline, resource allocation, and risk management strategies. Planning also involves creating a work breakdown structure (WBS) to break down the project into smaller, manageable components.

3. **Execution**:
   - In the execution phase, the project plan is put into action. Resources are allocated, tasks are assigned, and work begins. The project manager oversees the team's efforts, coordinates activities, and ensures that deliverables are being produced as planned. Effective communication and collaboration are crucial during this phase to

ensure that everyone is aligned and working towards the same goals. The project manager also monitors progress, manages changes, and addresses any issues that arise.

4. **Monitoring and Controlling**:
   - o This phase involves tracking the project's progress and performance. The project manager monitors key metrics, manages changes, and ensures that the project stays on track. Adjustments are made as necessary to address any issues or deviations from the plan. Regular status meetings and progress reports help keep stakeholders informed and engaged. Performance measurement techniques, such as earned value management (EVM), can be used to assess project performance and forecast future progress.

5. **Closing**:
   - o The closing phase marks the completion of the project. Key activities include finalizing deliverables, obtaining stakeholder approval, and conducting a project review. Lessons learned are documented, and the project is officially closed. The project manager ensures that all project documentation is complete, resources are released, and any remaining issues are resolved. A final project report is prepared, summarizing the project's outcomes, achievements, and lessons learned.

Understanding these foundational elements of project management will prepare you for more in-depth discussions in the subsequent chapters. By grasping the basics, you will be better equipped to plan, execute, and manage successful projects, no matter their size or complexity. Effective project management is a valuable skill that can lead to improved efficiency, better outcomes, and greater satisfaction in both personal and professional endeavours.

Chapter 2: Defining Your Project

Defining your project is the critical first step in the project management process. A well-defined project lays the foundation for success by setting clear objectives, identifying stakeholders, and outlining the scope. In this chapter, we will delve into the essential components of project definition: identifying project objectives and goals, understanding project scope, stakeholder identification and analysis, and creating a project charter.

Identifying Project Objectives and Goals

The first step in defining your project is to establish clear, concise objectives and goals. These serve as the guiding star for all project activities and decisions. Objectives and goals should be Specific, Measurable, Achievable, Relevant, and Time-bound (SMART). This framework ensures that your project has a clear direction and that progress can be tracked effectively.

SMART Criteria:

- **Specific**: Clearly define what you want to achieve. Avoid vague statements and focus on concrete outcomes.
- **Measurable**: Establish criteria for measuring progress and success. Quantifiable metrics help in tracking progress.
- **Achievable**: Set realistic goals that are attainable given the available resources and constraints.
- **Relevant**: Ensure that the objectives align with broader organizational or personal goals.
- **Time-bound**: Set a clear timeline for achieving the objectives, including deadlines and milestones.

Example of SMART Goals:

- Specific: Increase website traffic by 20%.
- Measurable: Track the number of visitors using web analytics tools.
- Achievable: Based on past performance, a 20% increase is realistic.
- Relevant: Aligns with the goal of expanding the online presence.
- Time-bound: Achieve this increase within six months.

Understanding Project Scope

The project scope defines the boundaries of the project, including what will be done and what will not be done. A well-defined scope sets clear expectations for deliverables and outcomes, helping to prevent scope creep, which is the tendency for project requirements to expand beyond the initial objectives.

Key Components of Project Scope:

- **Objectives**: What the project aims to achieve.
- **Deliverables**: Tangible or intangible outputs produced by the project.
- **Inclusions**: Specific tasks, activities, and features that are part of the project.
- **Exclusions**: Tasks, activities, and features that are not part of the project.
- **Constraints**: Limitations such as time, budget, and resources.
- **Assumptions**: Conditions believed to be true for planning purposes.

Creating a detailed scope statement involves working closely with stakeholders to understand their needs and expectations. This document becomes a reference point throughout the project lifecycle, guiding decisions and ensuring alignment with project goals.

Example of a Project Scope Statement:

- **Objective**: Develop a new mobile app for online shopping.
- **Deliverables**: Mobile app for iOS and Android, user documentation, and training materials.
- **Inclusions**: User authentication, product catalogue, shopping cart, payment gateway integration.
- **Exclusions**: Backend server infrastructure, marketing, and promotion of the app.
- **Constraints**: Budget of £100,000, project completion within six months.
- **Assumptions**: Internet access available for all users, existing payment gateway APIs available.

Stakeholder Identification and Analysis

Stakeholders are individuals or groups who have an interest in the outcome of the project. Identifying and understanding stakeholders is crucial for project success. Stakeholders can provide valuable insights, resources, and support, but they can also pose challenges if their expectations are not managed effectively.

Types of Stakeholders:

- **Primary Stakeholders**: Directly affected by the project, such as customers, clients, and team members.

- **Secondary Stakeholders**: Indirectly affected by the project, such as suppliers, regulatory bodies, and community groups.
- **Key Stakeholders**: Have significant influence over the project, such as sponsors, executives, and project managers.

Steps in Stakeholder Analysis:

1. **Identify Stakeholders**: List all individuals and groups who have an interest in the project.
2. **Assess Stakeholder Influence and Impact**: Evaluate the level of influence and impact each stakeholder has on the project.
3. **Understand Stakeholder Expectations**: Gather information on stakeholder needs, expectations, and concerns.
4. **Develop Stakeholder Engagement Strategies**: Plan how to engage and communicate with each stakeholder to manage their expectations and gain their support.

Example of Stakeholder Analysis:

- **Stakeholder**: Project Sponsor
  - **Influence**: High
  - **Impact**: High
  - **Expectations**: Successful project completion within budget and timeline.
  - **Engagement Strategy**: Regular progress updates, involvement in key decisions.
- **Stakeholder**: End Users
  - **Influence**: Medium
  - **Impact**: High

- Expectations: User-friendly interface, reliable performance.
- Engagement Strategy: User surveys, beta testing, feedback sessions.

Creating a Project Charter

A project charter is a formal document that authorizes the project and provides a high-level overview. It serves as a reference point throughout the project lifecycle and ensures that everyone involved understands the project's purpose, objectives, and scope.

Components of a Project Charter:

- **Project Title**: The name of the project.
- **Project Purpose**: A brief statement of why the project is being undertaken.
- **Objectives**: Specific goals that the project aims to achieve.
- **Scope**: A summary of what is included and excluded in the project.
- **Stakeholders**: Key individuals and groups involved in the project.
- **Deliverables**: Major outputs of the project.
- **Constraints**: Limitations such as time, budget, and resources.
- **Assumptions**: Conditions believed to be true for planning purposes.
- **Project Manager**: The person responsible for leading the project.
- **Authorization**: Formal approval from project sponsors or executives.

Example of a Project Charter:

- **Project Title**: Mobile App Development
- **Project Purpose**: To develop a new mobile app that enhances the online shopping experience.
- **Objectives**: Increase user engagement, improve customer satisfaction, and boost sales by 20% within the first year.
- **Scope**: Develop an iOS and Android app with features such as user authentication, product catalogue, shopping cart, and payment gateway integration.
- **Stakeholders**: Project Sponsor, Project Manager, Development Team, End Users.
- **Deliverables**: Mobile app for iOS and Android, user documentation, training materials.
- **Constraints**: Budget of £100,000, project completion within six months.
- **Assumptions**: Internet access available for all users, existing payment gateway APIs available.
- **Project Manager**: Jane Doe
- **Authorization**: Approved by John Smith, Executive Sponsor

Practical Steps for Defining Your Project

1. **Conduct Initial Research**: Gather preliminary information about the project's feasibility, potential challenges, and opportunities. This may involve market research, technical assessments, and consultations with stakeholders.
2. **Hold Stakeholder Meetings**: Organize meetings with key stakeholders to discuss their expectations, needs, and concerns. Use this information to shape the project's objectives and scope.
3. **Draft the Project Charter**: Create a draft of the project charter, including all essential components. Review the

draft with stakeholders to ensure alignment and address any concerns.

4. **Finalize and Approve the Project Charter**: Make necessary revisions based on stakeholder feedback. Obtain formal approval from the project sponsor or executive team to authorize the project.

5. **Communicate the Project Charter**: Share the approved project charter with all stakeholders and team members. Ensure that everyone understands the project's objectives, scope, and their roles and responsibilities.

Tips for Effective Project Definition

- **Be Clear and Specific**: Avoid vague language and ensure that objectives, scope, and deliverables are clearly defined. This helps prevent misunderstandings and sets clear expectations.

- **Engage Stakeholders Early**: Involve stakeholders in the project definition process to gain their support and ensure that their needs and expectations are considered.

- **Document Everything**: Keep thorough records of all discussions, decisions, and agreements. Documentation serves as a reference and helps resolve any disputes that may arise.

- **Stay Flexible**: Be prepared to make adjustments as new information becomes available or as stakeholder needs change. Flexibility is key to adapting to unforeseen challenges and opportunities.

- **Use Visual Aids**: Diagrams, charts, and other visual aids can help communicate complex information more effectively. Use these tools to enhance understanding and engagement.

By carefully defining your project, you set the stage for a successful execution. Clear objectives, a well-defined scope, and thorough stakeholder analysis provide the foundation for effective planning, execution, and monitoring. In the next chapter, we will explore the detailed planning process, including creating a project plan, developing a schedule, budgeting, and risk management planning.

Chapter 3: Planning Your Project (continued)

Budgeting (continued)

4. **Review and Adjust**: Review the budget with stakeholders and adjust as necessary to address any concerns or potential discrepancies. Ensure that the budget aligns with the overall project objectives and constraints.
5. **Monitor and Control**: Throughout the project, continuously monitor actual spending against the budget. Use project management software or tools to track expenses in real-time. Make adjustments as needed to stay within budget.

Example of a Project Budget:

Expense Category	Estimated Cost
Labor	£80,000
Equipment	£10,000
Materials	£5,000
Software Licenses	£2,000
Training	£3,000
Contingency (5%)	£5,000
Total	**£105,000**

Risk Management Planning

Risk management is an essential part of project planning that involves identifying, assessing, and mitigating risks that could potentially impact the project. Effective risk management helps minimize disruptions and ensures the project stays on track.

Steps to Develop a Risk Management Plan:

1. **Identify Risks**: Brainstorm potential risks that could affect the project. Consider technical, financial, environmental, and organizational risks. Engage stakeholders and team members to gather a comprehensive list of risks.
2. **Assess Risks**: Evaluate the likelihood and impact of each risk. Prioritize risks based on their potential to disrupt the project. Use a risk matrix to categorize risks as high, medium, or low.
3. **Develop Mitigation Strategies**: For each identified risk, develop strategies to mitigate or manage the risk. This may involve avoiding the risk, reducing its likelihood or impact, transferring the risk, or accepting the risk if it is within tolerable limits.
4. **Create a Risk Register**: Document all identified risks, their assessments, and mitigation strategies in a risk register. This register should be regularly updated and reviewed throughout the project.
5. **Monitor and Control Risks**: Continuously monitor risks and the effectiveness of mitigation strategies. Be prepared to adjust plans and take corrective actions as new risks emerge or existing risks change.

Example of a Risk Register:

Risk	Likelihood	Impact	Mitigation Strategy	Owner
Delay in app development	Medium	High	Add buffer time, allocate extra resources	Project Manager
Budget overrun	High	Medium	Monitor expenses closely, reduce	Finance Officer

			discretionary spending	
Technical issues	Low	High	Conduct thorough testing, have backup plans	Lead Developer
Resource availability	Medium	Medium	Cross-train team members, have contingency staffing	HR Manager

Practical Steps for Effective Planning

1. **Engage Stakeholders**: Involve stakeholders in the planning process to ensure their expectations are considered and to gain their support. Hold regular planning meetings to discuss progress and gather input.

2. **Use Project Management Tools**: Utilize project management software such as Microsoft Project, Trello, or Asana to create detailed plans, schedules, and budgets. These tools can help streamline planning activities and improve accuracy.

3. **Set Clear Milestones**: Define clear milestones and deliverables to track progress. Milestones serve as checkpoints to evaluate the project's status and make necessary adjustments.

4. **Regularly Review and Update Plans**: Plans should be living documents that are regularly reviewed and updated as new information becomes available or as project circumstances change. Schedule regular review sessions to ensure plans remain relevant and effective.

5. **Communicate Effectively**: Establish open lines of communication among all project participants. Ensure that everyone understands their roles and responsibilities and is aware of any changes to the plan.

Tips for Successful Project Planning

- **Start Early**: Begin planning as early as possible to allow ample time for thorough preparation. Early planning helps identify potential issues and address them before they become critical.
- **Be Realistic**: Set realistic expectations for timelines, budgets, and resources. Overly optimistic plans can lead to frustration and project failure.
- **Involve the Team**: Engage the project team in the planning process to leverage their expertise and gain their commitment. Team involvement fosters ownership and accountability.
- **Document Everything**: Keep detailed records of all planning activities, decisions, and assumptions. Documentation provides a reference and helps resolve disputes.
- **Plan for Contingencies**: Always have backup plans in place for key project components. Contingency planning ensures the project can continue smoothly in the face of unexpected challenges.
- **Focus on Critical Tasks**: Identify and prioritize critical tasks that have the most significant impact on the project's success. Ensure these tasks receive adequate attention and resources.

By investing time and effort in comprehensive project planning, you lay a solid foundation for successful project execution. A well-developed project plan, clear schedule, realistic budget, and proactive risk management approach will guide your project to a successful conclusion. In the next chapter, we will explore the execution phase, including how to allocate resources, manage the project team, and ensure effective communication throughout the project lifecycle.

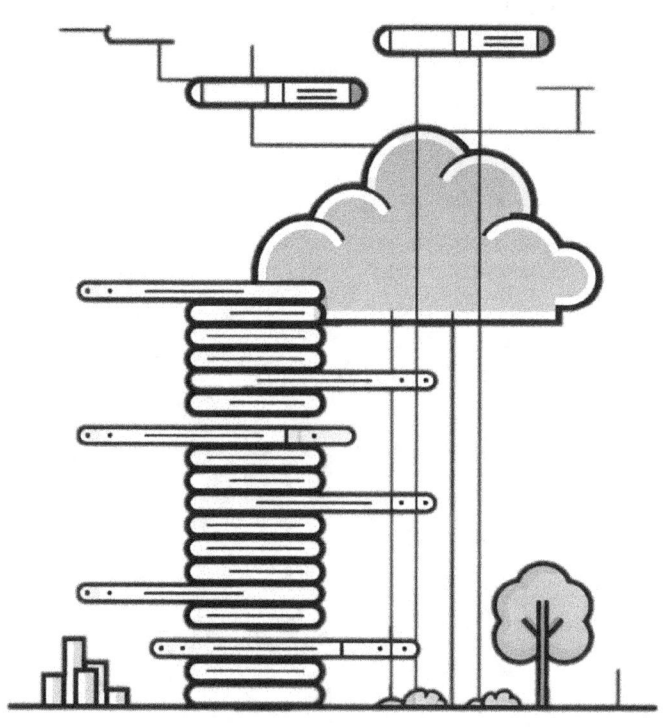

Chapter 4: Organizing Your Project

Organizing your project is crucial for ensuring that all elements come together smoothly and efficiently. This phase involves assembling your project team, defining roles and responsibilities, allocating resources, and establishing effective communication channels. Proper organization sets the stage for successful execution and helps prevent misunderstandings and delays.

Building Your Project Team

The success of a project largely depends on the people involved. Building a strong project team is essential for achieving your project goals. When selecting team members, consider their skills, experience, and how well they complement each other.

Steps to Build a Project Team:

1. **Identify Required Skills and Roles**: Determine the skills and expertise needed to complete the project. This includes technical skills, project management skills, and domain-specific knowledge. Identify the roles that need to be filled, such as project manager, developers, testers, and subject matter experts.
2. **Select Team Members**: Choose individuals who possess the required skills and experience. Consider their availability and willingness to commit to the project. Aim for a diverse team that brings different perspectives and strengths.
3. **Assign Roles and Responsibilities**: Clearly define each team member's role and responsibilities. Ensure that

everyone understands what is expected of them and how their work contributes to the project's success.

4. **Establish Team Norms and Expectations**: Set clear expectations for team behaviour, communication, and collaboration. Establish ground rules for meetings, decision-making, and conflict resolution.

5. **Build Team Cohesion**: Foster a sense of teamwork and collaboration by organizing team-building activities and encouraging open communication. A cohesive team is more likely to work well together and achieve project goals.

Example of a Project Team Structure:

Role	Responsibilities
Project Manager	Overall project coordination, stakeholder communication, risk management
Lead Developer	Technical leadership, code reviews, ensuring quality standards
Developer	Writing code, implementing features, debugging
Tester	Testing software, identifying and reporting bugs
Subject Matter Expert	Providing domain-specific knowledge and guidance
Business Analyst	Gathering requirements, documenting project scope
UX/UI Designer	Designing user interfaces, ensuring user experience standards

Defining Roles and Responsibilities

Clear roles and responsibilities are essential for effective project management. When team members know what is expected of them, they can focus on their tasks and contribute to the project's success. Define roles and responsibilities at the beginning of the project and communicate them to all team members.

Steps to Define Roles and Responsibilities:

1. **Identify Key Tasks and Deliverables**: List the key tasks and deliverables required to complete the project. Break down each task into smaller components if necessary.
2. **Assign Roles**: Assign each task to a specific role. Ensure that each role has a clear set of responsibilities and that there is no overlap or confusion.
3. **Document Responsibilities**: Create a responsibilities matrix that outlines who is responsible for each task. Include details such as the person's name, role, and specific duties.
4. **Communicate Expectations**: Share the responsibilities matrix with the entire team and ensure that everyone understands their roles. Address any questions or concerns that team members may have.

Example of a Responsibilities Matrix:

Task	Responsible Role	Specific Duties
Develop App Features	Lead Developer	Oversee development, conduct code reviews
Write Code	Developer	Implement features, debug code
Test Software	Tester	Perform testing, report bugs
Gather Requirements	Business Analyst	Conduct stakeholder interviews, document requirements

Design User Interface	UX/UI Designer	Create wireframes, design user interfaces
Manage Project Schedule	Project Manager	Update schedule, track progress
Provide Domain Knowledge	Subject Matter Expert	Advise on industry standards, review deliverables

Allocating Resources

Effective resource allocation ensures that your project has the necessary people, equipment, and materials to complete tasks on time and within budget. Proper resource management helps avoid bottlenecks and ensures a smooth workflow.

Steps to Allocate Resources:

1. **Identify Resource Requirements**: Determine the resources needed for each task, including personnel, equipment, materials, and budget. Consider factors such as availability, skill levels, and capacity.
2. **Assign Resources to Tasks**: Allocate resources based on their availability and suitability for the task. Ensure that resources are not over-allocated and that there is a balance between workload and capacity.
3. **Create a Resource Plan**: Develop a resource plan that outlines how resources will be allocated throughout the project. This plan should include a schedule, resource assignments, and a budget.
4. **Monitor Resource Usage**: Continuously monitor resource usage to ensure that resources are being used effectively and efficiently. Make adjustments as needed to address any issues or changes in availability.

5. **Manage Resource Conflicts**: Address any resource conflicts or constraints that arise during the project. This may involve reallocating resources, adjusting timelines, or negotiating with stakeholders.

Example of a Resource Plan:

Task	Resource	Allocation (Hours)	Start Date	End Date
Develop App Features	Lead Developer	120	Feb 12	May 12
Write Code	Developer 1	100	Feb 12	May 12
Write Code	Developer 2	100	Feb 12	May 12
Test Software	Tester	60	May 13	Jun 12
Gather Requirements	Business Analyst	40	Jan 15	Jan 28
Design User Interface	UX/UI Designer	80	Jan 29	Feb 11
Manage Project Schedule	Project Manager	20	Throughout	Throughout
Provide Domain Knowledge	Subject Matter Expert	30	Throughout	Throughout

Establishing Effective Communication Channels

Effective communication is vital for the success of any project. It ensures that everyone is informed, aligned, and able to collaborate effectively. Establishing clear communication channels and protocols helps prevent misunderstandings and keeps the project on track.

Steps to Establish Communication Channels:

1. **Identify Stakeholders and Communication Needs**: Determine who needs to be informed about the project's progress and how often. Identify key stakeholders, team members, and other relevant parties.
2. **Define Communication Methods**: Choose the most appropriate methods for communication, such as email, meetings, project management software, or instant messaging. Consider the preferences and availability of stakeholders.
3. **Set Communication Protocols**: Establish guidelines for how and when communication will occur. This includes setting meeting schedules, report formats, and response times.
4. **Create a Communication Plan**: Develop a communication plan that outlines the communication methods, protocols, and schedules. Ensure that the plan is shared with all stakeholders and team members.
5. **Monitor and Adjust**: Continuously monitor the effectiveness of communication channels and make adjustments as needed. Seek feedback from stakeholders to identify areas for improvement.

Example of a Communication Plan:

Communication Method	Frequency	Audience	Purpose
Weekly Team Meetings	Weekly	Project Team	Discuss progress, address issues,

			plan tasks
Bi-Weekly Progress Reports	Bi-weekly	Stakeholders	Provide status updates, highlight achievements
Project Management Software	Ongoing	Project Team	Real-time updates, task assignments
Monthly Steering Committee Meetings	Monthly	Steering Committee	Review project status, make strategic decisions
Email Updates	As Needed	All Stakeholders	Share important information, urgent updates

Practical Steps for Organizing Your Project

1. **Conduct a Kick-off Meeting**: Hold a kick-off meeting with the project team and stakeholders to review the project plan, roles, responsibilities, and communication protocols. This meeting sets the tone for the project and ensures everyone is aligned.
2. **Set Up Project Management Tools**: Utilize project management software such as Microsoft Project, Trello, or Asana to organize tasks, track progress, and facilitate communication. These tools help streamline project management activities and improve efficiency.
3. **Establish Regular Check-Ins**: Schedule regular check-ins with the project team and stakeholders to review progress, address any issues, and make necessary adjustments. Regular communication helps keep the project on track and ensures that everyone is informed.

4. **Document Processes and Procedures**: Document all project processes and procedures to provide a reference for the team. This includes task workflows, communication protocols, and quality standards. Documentation helps maintain consistency and ensures that everyone follows the same procedures.
5. **Foster a Collaborative Environment**: Encourage open communication and collaboration among team members. Create a supportive environment where team members feel comfortable sharing ideas, asking questions, and providing feedback.
6. **Monitor and Adjust**: Continuously monitor the project's progress and make adjustments as needed. Be proactive in addressing any issues or changes in scope, resources, or timelines. Regular monitoring helps identify potential problems early and allows for timely interventions.

Tips for Successful Project Organization

- **Be Clear and Concise**: Clearly communicate roles, responsibilities, and expectations to all team members. Avoid ambiguity and ensure that everyone understands their tasks and how they contribute to the project's success.
- **Prioritize Tasks**: Focus on high-priority tasks that have the most significant impact on the project's success. Ensure that critical tasks receive adequate attention and resources.
- **Encourage Collaboration**: Foster a collaborative environment where team members can work together effectively. Encourage open communication, idea sharing, and mutual support.
- **Stay Flexible**: Be prepared to adapt to changes in scope, resources, or timelines. Flexibility allows you to respond to

unforeseen challenges and take advantage of new opportunities.

- **Recognize and Reward Contributions**: Acknowledge the efforts and contributions of team members. Recognition and rewards help motivate the team and build a positive working environment.
- **Maintain Transparency**: Keep stakeholders informed about the project's progress, challenges, and successes. Transparency builds trust and ensures that everyone is aligned with the project's goals.

By organizing your project effectively, you create a solid foundation for successful execution. Clear roles and responsibilities, efficient resource allocation, and effective communication channels help ensure that all project activities are coordinated and aligned with the overall objectives. In the next chapter, we will explore the execution phase, including how to allocate resources, manage the project team, and ensure effective communication throughout the project lifecycle.

Chapter 5: Leading Your Project Team

Leading a project team requires a unique blend of management skills, leadership qualities, and effective communication strategies. As a project manager, your role extends beyond planning and organizing; you must also inspire, motivate, and guide your team to achieve the project's objectives. This chapter will explore the differences between leadership and management, techniques for motivating and guiding your team, strategies for effective communication, and approaches to conflict resolution and problem-solving.

Leadership vs. Management in Project Management

While leadership and management are often used interchangeably, they represent distinct skills and approaches that are both essential for successful project management.

Management involves planning, organizing, and coordinating resources to achieve specific goals. Managers focus on processes, systems, and procedures to ensure that tasks are completed efficiently and effectively. Key management activities include setting objectives, allocating resources, monitoring progress, and ensuring compliance with standards and regulations.

Leadership, on the other hand, involves inspiring and motivating people to achieve their full potential and work towards a common vision. Leaders focus on influencing, guiding, and supporting their team members. Key leadership activities include setting a clear vision, building trust, fostering collaboration, and encouraging innovation.

Key Differences Between Leadership and Management:

- **Focus**: Management focuses on processes and tasks, while leadership focuses on people and relationships.
- **Approach**: Managers plan and organize, while leaders inspire and motivate.
- **Goal**: Management aims to achieve specific objectives efficiently, while leadership aims to create a shared vision and inspire others to pursue it.
- **Style**: Managers tend to be more directive and structured, while leaders tend to be more flexible and adaptive.

Effective project managers need to balance both leadership and management skills. They must be able to plan and organize the project while also inspiring and motivating their team to achieve the project's goals.

Motivating and Guiding Your Team

Motivating your team is crucial for maintaining high levels of performance and ensuring project success. A motivated team is more engaged, productive, and committed to achieving project objectives. Here are some strategies for motivating and guiding your team:

1. **Set Clear Goals and Expectations**: Clearly communicate the project's objectives and the expected outcomes. Ensure that each team member understands their role and how their work contributes to the overall success of the project.
2. **Provide Autonomy and Empowerment**: Give team members the autonomy to make decisions and take ownership of their tasks. Empowering your team fosters a sense of responsibility and encourages innovation.

3. **Offer Recognition and Rewards**: Acknowledge and reward the efforts and achievements of your team members. Recognition can be in the form of verbal praise, written commendations, or tangible rewards such as bonuses or gifts.
4. **Create a Positive Work Environment**: Foster a supportive and inclusive work environment where team members feel valued and respected. Encourage open communication, collaboration, and mutual support.
5. **Provide Opportunities for Growth and Development**: Invest in the professional development of your team members. Offer training, mentoring, and opportunities for career advancement. Supporting your team's growth enhances their skills and increases their commitment to the project.
6. **Lead by Example**: Demonstrate the behaviours and attitudes you expect from your team. Show dedication, integrity, and a strong work ethic. Leading by example sets a positive tone and inspires your team to follow suit.

Effective Communication Strategies

Effective communication is the foundation of successful project management. It ensures that information flows smoothly, team members are aligned, and stakeholders are kept informed. Here are some strategies for effective communication:

1. **Establish Clear Communication Channels**: Define the communication channels and methods that will be used throughout the project. This can include meetings, emails, project management software, and instant messaging.
2. **Set Regular Communication Cadences**: Schedule regular check-ins and updates to keep the team and stakeholders informed about the project's progress. Regular

communication helps address issues early and keeps everyone aligned.

3. **Be Clear and Concise**: Communicate clearly and concisely to avoid misunderstandings. Use simple language and provide specific information. Avoid jargon and complex terminology that may confuse team members.

4. **Active Listening**: Practice active listening by paying attention to what others are saying, asking clarifying questions, and providing feedback. Active listening helps build trust and ensures that everyone's perspectives are heard.

5. **Use Visual Aids**: Use diagrams, charts, and other visual aids to enhance understanding and engagement. Visual aids can help clarify complex information and make it easier for team members to grasp key concepts.

6. **Encourage Open Communication**: Create an environment where team members feel comfortable sharing ideas, asking questions, and providing feedback. Encourage open and honest communication to foster collaboration and innovation.

7. **Adapt Communication Style**: Tailor your communication style to suit the needs of different team members and stakeholders. Some people may prefer detailed written reports, while others may prefer brief verbal updates. Adapt your communication to ensure it is effective for your audience.

Conflict Resolution and Problem-Solving

Conflicts are inevitable in any project, but effective conflict resolution and problem-solving can help maintain a positive team dynamic and keep the project on track. Here are some strategies for resolving conflicts and addressing problems:

1. **Identify the Root Cause**: Understand the underlying causes of the conflict or problem. This may involve talking to the parties involved, gathering information, and analysing the situation.
2. **Encourage Open Dialogue**: Create a safe space for team members to express their concerns and perspectives. Encourage open dialogue and active listening to understand different viewpoints.
3. **Focus on Interests, Not Positions**: Focus on the underlying interests and needs of the parties involved, rather than their positions. This approach helps identify mutually beneficial solutions.
4. **Collaborate on Solutions**: Work with the parties involved to brainstorm and evaluate potential solutions. Encourage collaboration and creativity to find the best possible resolution.
5. **Mediation and Facilitation**: If the conflict cannot be resolved through direct dialogue, consider involving a neutral third party to mediate or facilitate the discussion. A mediator can help guide the conversation and ensure that all parties are heard.
6. **Document Agreements**: Once a resolution is reached, document the agreement and ensure that all parties understand and agree to the terms. This helps prevent future misunderstandings and ensures accountability.
7. **Monitor and Follow-Up**: Monitor the situation to ensure that the resolution is being implemented and that the conflict does not reoccur. Follow up with the parties involved to address any ongoing concerns.

Practical Steps for Leading Your Project Team

1. **Conduct a Team Kick-off Meeting**: Hold a kick-off meeting to introduce team members, review the project plan, and

set expectations. Use this meeting to build rapport and establish a positive team dynamic.

2. **Set Clear Goals and Milestones**: Define clear goals and milestones for the project and communicate them to the team. Ensure that everyone understands what needs to be achieved and by when.

3. **Establish a Feedback Loop**: Create a feedback loop where team members can share their progress, challenges, and suggestions. Regular feedback helps identify issues early and fosters continuous improvement.

4. **Provide Regular Updates**: Keep the team and stakeholders informed with regular updates on the project's progress. Use status reports, meetings, and project management software to provide timely information.

5. **Address Issues Promptly**: Address any issues or conflicts promptly to prevent them from escalating. Use conflict resolution and problem-solving strategies to find effective solutions.

6. **Celebrate Successes**: Celebrate project milestones and successes to recognize the team's hard work and boost morale. Celebrations can be small, such as verbal recognition in meetings, or larger, such as team outings or rewards.

7. **Encourage Professional Development**: Support the professional development of your team members by providing training, mentoring, and opportunities for growth. Investing in your team's development enhances their skills and commitment to the project.

Tips for Successful Team Leadership

- **Build Trust**: Foster a culture of trust by being transparent, reliable, and supportive. Trust is the foundation of strong team relationships and effective collaboration.
- **Empower Your Team**: Empower team members to take ownership of their tasks and make decisions. Empowered teams are more motivated and engaged.
- **Be Approachable**: Be approachable and available to your team. Encourage them to come to you with questions, concerns, and ideas.
- **Lead with Empathy**: Understand and consider the perspectives and needs of your team members. Empathetic leadership helps build strong relationships and a supportive work environment.
- **Stay Positive**: Maintain a positive attitude, even in the face of challenges. Positivity is contagious and can help keep the team motivated and focused on solutions.

By leading your project team effectively, you can inspire, motivate, and guide your team to achieve the project's objectives. Balancing leadership and management skills, fostering a positive work environment, and maintaining clear communication are key to successful project leadership. In the next chapter, we will explore the execution phase, including how to allocate resources, manage the project team, and ensure effective communication throughout the project lifecycle.

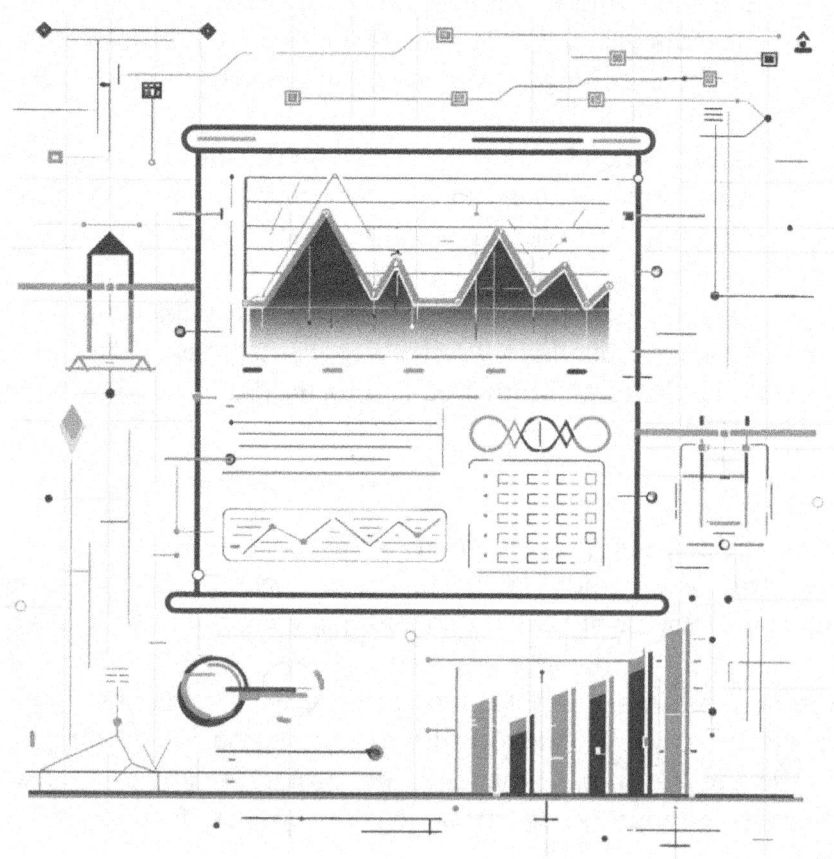

Chapter 6: Controlling and Monitoring Your Project

Controlling and monitoring your project is essential to ensure that it stays on track and meets its objectives. This phase involves tracking progress, managing changes, maintaining quality, and communicating with stakeholders. Effective control and monitoring allow you to identify issues early, make necessary adjustments, and keep the project aligned with its goals. In this chapter, we will explore the key activities involved in controlling and monitoring a project.

Tracking Project Progress

Tracking project progress involves regularly reviewing the status of tasks, milestones, and deliverables to ensure that the project is moving according to plan. Accurate tracking provides insights into the project's performance and helps identify any deviations from the plan.

Steps to Track Project Progress:

1. **Establish Baselines**: Set performance baselines for scope, schedule, and budget. These baselines serve as reference points to measure progress and performance.
2. **Monitor Key Performance Indicators (KPIs)**: Identify and monitor KPIs that are relevant to your project. KPIs are metrics that provide insights into the project's performance, such as task completion rates, budget variance, and resource utilization.
3. **Use Project Management Tools**: Utilize project management software to track progress in real-time. Tools

like Microsoft Project, Trello, or Asana can help visualize progress, manage tasks, and monitor deadlines.

4. **Conduct Regular Status Meetings**: Hold regular status meetings with the project team to review progress, discuss challenges, and plan next steps. These meetings provide an opportunity for team members to share updates and address any issues.

5. **Update Progress Reports**: Create and update progress reports that summarize the project's status. These reports should include information on completed tasks, upcoming activities, and any deviations from the plan.

Example of a Progress Report:

Task	Status	Completion (%)	Comments
Develop App Features	In Progress	60%	On track, minor delays in UI design
Write Code	In Progress	50%	Backend integration in progress
Test Software	Not Started	0%	Scheduled to start next week
Gather Requirements	Completed	100%	Stakeholder approval received
Design User Interface	In Progress	70%	Final revisions needed

Managing Changes

Change is inevitable in any project, and managing changes effectively is crucial for maintaining control. Change management involves identifying, assessing, and approving changes to the project scope, schedule, or budget.

Steps to Manage Changes:

1. **Identify Change Requests**: Encourage team members and stakeholders to submit change requests when they identify necessary changes. Change requests should include a description of the change, its impact, and the reason for the change.
2. **Assess Change Impact**: Evaluate the impact of the change on the project's scope, schedule, budget, and quality. Consider both the short-term and long-term effects of the change.
3. **Approve or Reject Changes**: Convene a change control board (CCB) or a similar decision-making body to review and approve or reject change requests. The CCB should include key stakeholders and project team members.
4. **Implement Approved Changes**: If a change request is approved, update the project plan, schedule, and budget to reflect the change. Communicate the change to the project team and stakeholders.
5. **Track and Document Changes**: Maintain a change log to track all change requests, their status, and their impact on the project. Documenting changes helps ensure transparency and accountability.

Example of a Change Log:

Change ID	Description	Impact	Status	Approval Date	Comments
CHG-001	Add new payment gateway	Schedule delay (2 weeks)	Approved	Jan 15	High priority feature
CHG-002	Modify user	Budget increase	Pending		Awaiting stakeholde

	interface design	(£5,000)			r review
CHG-003	Extend testing phase	Schedul e delay (1 week)	Approve d	Jan 22	Necessary for quality assurance

Maintaining Quality

Quality management ensures that the project's deliverables meet the required standards and satisfy stakeholder expectations. Maintaining quality involves both quality assurance (QA) and quality control (QC) activities.

Quality Assurance (QA) focuses on preventing defects by implementing processes and standards that ensure quality throughout the project lifecycle.

Quality Control (QC) involves inspecting and testing deliverables to identify and correct defects.

Steps to Maintain Quality:

1. **Define Quality Criteria**: Establish clear quality criteria and standards for the project's deliverables. Quality criteria should be measurable and align with stakeholder expectations.
2. **Implement Quality Processes**: Develop and implement quality processes and procedures to ensure that tasks are performed consistently and meet the required standards. This may include checklists, templates, and best practices.
3. **Conduct Regular Inspections and Tests**: Perform regular inspections and tests to verify that deliverables meet the

quality criteria. This may involve peer reviews, code reviews, user testing, and performance testing.

4. **Document Quality Issues**: Record any quality issues or defects that are identified during inspections and tests. Use a defect tracking system to document, prioritize, and resolve quality issues.

5. **Review and Improve**: Continuously review and improve quality processes and procedures based on feedback and lessons learned. Implement corrective actions to address recurring quality issues.

Example of a Quality Control Checklist:

Deliverable	Quality Criteria	Inspection Method	Status	Comments
Mobile App UI	Consistency with design guidelines	Visual inspection	Approved	Minor adjustments needed
Payment Gateway	Successful transaction processing	Functional testing	Approved	Passed all test cases
User Documentation	Clarity and completeness	Peer review	Approved	Feedback incorporated
Backend Integration	Performance and reliability	Load testing	In Progress	Further optimization required

Communicating with Stakeholders

Effective communication with stakeholders is essential for maintaining transparency, managing expectations, and ensuring project success. Regular communication helps keep stakeholders informed about the project's progress, challenges, and achievements.

Steps to Communicate with Stakeholders:

1. **Identify Stakeholder Needs**: Understand the information needs and preferences of each stakeholder. Tailor your communication approach to meet their specific requirements.
2. **Develop a Communication Plan**: Create a communication plan that outlines the frequency, methods, and content of communication with stakeholders. Ensure that the plan addresses all key stakeholders and their information needs.
3. **Provide Regular Updates**: Share regular updates on the project's progress, including status reports, meeting minutes, and performance metrics. Use multiple communication channels to ensure that stakeholders receive timely information.
4. **Address Stakeholder Concerns**: Listen to stakeholder concerns and address them promptly. Provide clear explanations and updates on how concerns are being addressed.
5. **Gather Feedback**: Solicit feedback from stakeholders on the project's progress and communication effectiveness. Use feedback to make improvements and ensure that stakeholders remain engaged and satisfied.

Example of a Stakeholder Communication Plan:

Communication Method	Frequency	Audience	Purpose
Weekly Status Reports	Weekly	Project Team	Provide progress updates, highlight issues
Monthly Steering Committee Meetings	Monthly	Steering Committee	Review project status, make strategic

			decisions
Bi-Weekly Stakeholder Updates	Bi-weekly	Stakeholders	Inform stakeholders of progress, gather feedback
Project Management Software	Ongoing	Project Team	Real-time updates, task assignments
Email Newsletters	Monthly	All Stakeholders	Share important information, celebrate milestones

Practical Steps for Controlling and Monitoring Your Project

1. **Set Up Monitoring Tools**: Utilize project management software and tools to monitor progress, track performance, and manage changes. Tools like Microsoft Project, Jira, or Asana can help streamline monitoring activities.
2. **Conduct Regular Reviews**: Schedule regular review sessions with the project team and stakeholders to assess progress, identify issues, and make necessary adjustments. Regular reviews help maintain alignment and ensure that the project stays on track.
3. **Implement Change Control Processes**: Establish clear processes for managing changes to the project scope, schedule, and budget. Use a change control board (CCB) to review and approve change requests.
4. **Perform Quality Assurance Activities**: Implement quality assurance processes to ensure that tasks are performed consistently and meet the required standards. Conduct regular inspections and tests to verify the quality of deliverables.

5. **Maintain Open Communication**: Keep communication channels open and ensure that stakeholders are informed about the project's progress, challenges, and achievements. Use regular updates, status reports, and meetings to keep everyone aligned.
6. **Document Lessons Learned**: Document lessons learned throughout the project to identify areas for improvement and share best practices. Use lessons learned to make continuous improvements and avoid repeating mistakes.

Tips for Successful Control and Monitoring

- **Be Proactive**: Anticipate potential issues and take preventive actions to avoid disruptions. Proactive monitoring helps identify problems early and allows for timely interventions.
- **Stay Flexible**: Be prepared to adapt to changes in scope, resources, or timelines. Flexibility allows you to respond to unforeseen challenges and take advantage of new opportunities.
- **Maintain Accuracy**: Ensure that tracking and reporting are accurate and up-to-date. Accurate data provides a reliable basis for decision-making and helps maintain stakeholder confidence.
- **Foster Collaboration**: Encourage collaboration and teamwork among project team members. Collaborative efforts help identify issues early and develop effective solutions.
- **Focus on Continuous Improvement**: Continuously review and improve project processes based on feedback and lessons learned. Continuous improvement helps enhance project performance and outcomes.

By effectively controlling and monitoring your project, you can ensure that it stays on track and meets its objectives. Regular tracking, proactive change management, quality assurance, and clear communication are key to successful project control and monitoring. In the next chapter, we will explore the closing phase of the project, including finalizing deliverables, conducting project reviews, and celebrating success.

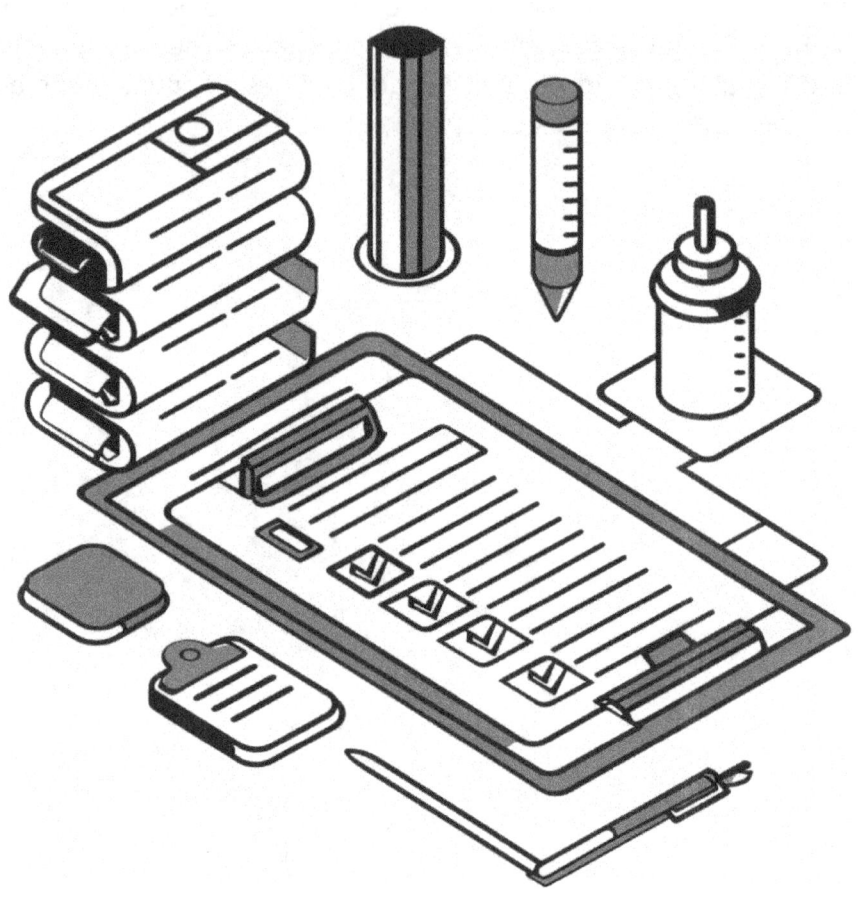

Chapter 7: Closing Your Project

The closing phase marks the culmination of your project. This phase involves finalizing all project activities, delivering the completed product to the client, obtaining stakeholder approval, and conducting a thorough review to document lessons learned. Effective project closure ensures that all objectives are met and that the team can transition smoothly to future projects. In this chapter, we will explore the key activities involved in closing a project.

Finalizing Deliverables

Finalizing deliverables involves ensuring that all project outputs are complete, meet quality standards, and are ready for handover to the client or stakeholders. This step is critical for verifying that the project objectives have been achieved and that the deliverables meet the requirements.

Steps to Finalize Deliverables:

1. **Review Deliverables**: Conduct a thorough review of all deliverables to ensure they meet the specified requirements and quality standards. This may involve final inspections, testing, and verification.
2. **Obtain Stakeholder Approval**: Present the deliverables to stakeholders for approval. Provide documentation and evidence to demonstrate that the deliverables meet the agreed-upon criteria.
3. **Make Necessary Adjustments**: Address any feedback or requests for changes from stakeholders. Make necessary

adjustments to the deliverables to ensure they meet stakeholder expectations.

4. **Document Final Deliverables**: Prepare detailed documentation for each deliverable, including user manuals, technical specifications, and other relevant materials. Documentation helps ensure that stakeholders can effectively use and maintain the deliverables.

5. **Handover Deliverables**: Officially hand over the completed deliverables to the client or stakeholders. Ensure that they have all the necessary information and resources to use the deliverables effectively.

Example of Deliverable Finalization:

Deliverable	Review Method	Status	Comments
Mobile App	Functional Testing	Approved	Passed all test cases
User Documentation	Peer Review	Approved	Feedback incorporated
Training Materials	Stakeholder Review	Approved	Final revisions completed
Backend Integration	Performance Testing	Approved	Meets performance criteria

Conducting a Project Review

A project review is a critical step in the closing phase that involves evaluating the project's performance, documenting lessons learned, and identifying areas for improvement. The review helps capture valuable insights that can be applied to future projects.

Steps to Conduct a Project Review:

1. **Gather Feedback**: Collect feedback from team members, stakeholders, and clients. Use surveys, interviews, and meetings to gather insights on what worked well and what could be improved.
2. **Analyse Project Performance**: Evaluate the project's performance against the original objectives, scope, schedule, and budget. Identify any deviations and analyse the reasons for these deviations.
3. **Document Lessons Learned**: Create a comprehensive lessons learned document that captures key insights from the project. Include information on successful practices, challenges encountered, and recommendations for future projects.
4. **Identify Best Practices**: Highlight best practices that contributed to the project's success. Share these practices with the project team and other relevant parties to promote continuous improvement.
5. **Conduct a Final Team Meeting**: Hold a final team meeting to discuss the project's outcomes, celebrate successes, and address any remaining issues. Use this meeting to foster a sense of closure and acknowledge the team's contributions.

Example of a Lessons Learned Document:

Category	Insight/Observation	Recommendation
Planning	Detailed project planning helped avoid scope creep	Continue using comprehensive planning tools
Communication	Regular status meetings improved team alignment	Maintain regular meetings for future projects
Risk Management	Early risk identification mitigated potential	Implement proactive risk management

	issues	practices
Quality Control	Thorough testing ensured high-quality deliverables	Continue rigorous testing procedures

Celebrating Success

Celebrating success is an important aspect of project closure that helps recognize the hard work and achievements of the project team. Celebrations boost morale, reinforce a positive work culture, and motivate team members for future projects.

Ways to Celebrate Success:

1. **Public Recognition**: Acknowledge the contributions of team members in a public forum, such as a company-wide meeting or announcement. Public recognition reinforces the value of the team's efforts.
2. **Awards and Certificates**: Present team members with awards or certificates of appreciation. Tangible recognition provides a lasting reminder of their accomplishments.
3. **Team Outing or Event**: Organize a team outing or event to celebrate the project's success. This could be a team lunch, dinner, or a fun activity that allows team members to relax and enjoy their success.
4. **Bonus or Incentive**: Offer financial incentives, such as bonuses or gift cards, to reward team members for their hard work. Financial rewards provide a tangible benefit and encourage continued high performance.
5. **Personal Thank-You Notes**: Write personalized thank-you notes to each team member, expressing your appreciation for their contributions. Personalized notes add a personal touch and show genuine gratitude.

Transitioning to Future Projects

Once the project is officially closed, it's important to ensure a smooth transition to future projects. This involves archiving project documentation, releasing resources, and preparing for new assignments.

Steps for Transitioning to Future Projects:

1. **Archive Project Documentation**: Organize and archive all project documentation, including plans, reports, deliverables, and lessons learned. Ensure that documentation is easily accessible for future reference.
2. **Release Resources**: Release project resources, including personnel, equipment, and materials. Ensure that team members are reassigned to new projects or tasks as appropriate.
3. **Conduct Exit Interviews**: Hold exit interviews with team members to gather feedback on their experience and identify areas for improvement. Use this feedback to enhance future project management practices.
4. **Prepare for New Projects**: Begin planning for new projects by reviewing lessons learned and applying best practices. Ensure that the team is equipped with the knowledge and resources needed for upcoming assignments.
5. **Maintain Communication**: Keep lines of communication open with stakeholders and team members as you transition to new projects. Regular updates and check-ins help maintain engagement and continuity.

Practical Steps for Project Closure

1. **Conduct a Final Walkthrough**: Perform a final walkthrough of all project deliverables to ensure they

meet the specified requirements and quality standards. Address any remaining issues or discrepancies.

2. **Obtain Formal Acceptance**: Secure formal acceptance of the project deliverables from the client or stakeholders. This involves obtaining signatures on acceptance documents and confirming that all criteria have been met.

3. **Prepare a Project Closure Report**: Create a project closure report that summarizes the project's outcomes, performance, and lessons learned. Share this report with stakeholders and relevant parties.

4. **Update Project Management Systems**: Update project management systems and tools to reflect the project's completion. Close out any remaining tasks, update schedules, and archive relevant data.

5. **Celebrate Achievements**: Organize a celebration to recognize the team's hard work and accomplishments. Use this opportunity to boost morale and reinforce a positive work culture.

6. **Reflect and Learn**: Take time to reflect on the project's successes and challenges. Use this reflection to identify areas for improvement and develop strategies for enhancing future project performance.

Tips for Successful Project Closure

- **Be Thorough**: Ensure that all project activities are completed and documented. Thorough closure helps prevent issues from arising after the project is completed.
- **Communicate Clearly**: Keep stakeholders informed throughout the closure process. Clear communication helps manage expectations and ensures a smooth handover.
- **Acknowledge Contributions**: Recognize and celebrate the contributions of team members. Acknowledging their

efforts fosters a positive work environment and motivates them for future projects.

- **Learn and Improve**: Use the project closure phase as an opportunity to learn and improve. Document lessons learned and apply best practices to future projects.
- **Plan for the Future**: Prepare for future projects by reviewing lessons learned and applying insights gained from the current project. Continuous improvement is key to long-term success.

By effectively closing your project, you ensure that all objectives are met, stakeholders are satisfied, and the team can transition smoothly to future assignments. Finalizing deliverables, conducting a thorough project review, celebrating success, and planning for future projects are essential components of successful project closure. In the next chapter, we will explore additional tips and tricks for successful project management, including practical advice for staying organized, managing time effectively, and using tools and software to enhance project performance.

Chapter 8: Tips and Tricks for Successful Project Management

Successful project management requires a combination of skills, strategies, and tools to ensure that projects are completed on time, within budget, and to the satisfaction of stakeholders. This chapter provides practical tips and tricks to help you stay organized, manage time effectively, and utilize tools and software to enhance project performance.

Practical Advice for Staying Organized

Staying organized is essential for managing multiple tasks, deadlines, and team members. Here are some practical tips to help you maintain organization throughout the project lifecycle:

1. **Use a Centralized Project Management Tool**: Utilize a project management tool like Trello, Asana, or Microsoft Project to keep all project information in one place. These tools allow you to create task lists, set deadlines, assign responsibilities, and track progress.
2. **Create a Project Calendar**: Develop a project calendar to visualize key milestones, deadlines, and events. Use color-coding to differentiate between tasks, phases, and team members. Update the calendar regularly to reflect any changes.
3. **Organize Documents and Files**: Maintain a well-organized system for storing project documents and files. Use cloud storage solutions like Google Drive, Dropbox, or SharePoint to ensure easy access and collaboration. Create folders and subfolders to categorize documents by type, phase, or team member.

4. **Use Checklists**: Create checklists for tasks and activities to ensure nothing is overlooked. Checklists help break down complex tasks into manageable steps and provide a sense of accomplishment as items are completed.
5. **Set Priorities**: Prioritize tasks based on their importance and urgency. Use the Eisenhower Matrix to categorize tasks into four quadrants: urgent and important, important but not urgent, urgent but not important, and neither urgent nor important. Focus on high-priority tasks first.
6. **Schedule Regular Review Meetings**: Hold regular review meetings with the project team to discuss progress, address challenges, and plan next steps. Use these meetings to stay aligned and ensure everyone is on the same page.
7. **Document Everything**: Keep detailed records of all project activities, decisions, and communications. Documentation provides a reference for future projects and helps resolve any disputes or misunderstandings.

Time Management Techniques

Effective time management is crucial for ensuring that projects stay on track and meet deadlines. Here are some time management techniques to help you manage your time and the team's time more effectively:

1. **The Pomodoro Technique**: Break work into intervals, typically 25 minutes, followed by a short break. This technique helps maintain focus and productivity while preventing burnout.
2. **Time Blocking**: Allocate specific blocks of time for different tasks or activities. Schedule these blocks on your calendar and stick to them as much as possible. Time

blocking helps ensure that you dedicate sufficient time to important tasks.

3. **Prioritize Tasks with the ABCDE Method**: Categorize tasks into five priority levels:
   - A: Must-do tasks with serious consequences if not completed.
   - B: Should-do tasks with mild consequences if not completed.
   - C: Nice-to-do tasks with no consequences if not completed.
   - D: Delegate tasks to others.
   - E: Eliminate tasks that are not necessary.

4. **Set SMART Goals**: Ensure that your goals are Specific, Measurable, Achievable, Relevant, and Time-bound. SMART goals provide clear direction and help you stay focused on what needs to be accomplished.

5. **Use the 80/20 Rule (Pareto Principle)**: Focus on the 20% of tasks that will yield 80% of the results. Identify the most critical tasks that contribute to your project's success and prioritize them.

6. **Limit Multitasking**: Focus on one task at a time to improve productivity and reduce errors. Multitasking can lead to decreased efficiency and increased stress.

7. **Take Regular Breaks**: Schedule regular breaks to rest and recharge. Breaks help prevent burnout and maintain high levels of productivity throughout the day.

Leveraging Tools and Software

Project management tools and software can significantly enhance your ability to manage projects effectively. Here are some popular tools and how they can be used:

1. **Trello**: A visual project management tool that uses boards, lists, and cards to organize tasks. Trello is great for managing tasks, tracking progress, and collaborating with team members.
2. **Asana**: A comprehensive project management tool that allows you to create tasks, set deadlines, assign responsibilities, and track progress. Asana's timeline feature helps visualize project schedules.
3. **Microsoft Project**: A robust project management software that offers advanced scheduling, resource management, and reporting capabilities. Microsoft Project is ideal for complex projects with multiple dependencies.
4. **Jira**: A tool designed for agile project management, particularly in software development. Jira supports sprint planning, issue tracking, and real-time collaboration.
5. **Slack**: A communication platform that facilitates team collaboration through channels, direct messages, and file sharing. Slack integrates with various project management tools to streamline communication.
6. **Google Workspace**: A suite of productivity tools, including Google Drive, Docs, Sheets, and Calendar. Google Workspace supports document collaboration, file sharing, and scheduling.
7. **Miro**: An online collaborative whiteboard platform that allows teams to brainstorm, plan, and visualize ideas. Miro is useful for remote teams and visual project planning.

Example of How to Use Trello for Project Management:

- **Create a Board**: Set up a board for your project with lists representing different phases or categories, such as "To Do," "In Progress," and "Completed."

- **Add Cards**: Create cards for individual tasks or deliverables. Assign due dates, labels, and team members to each card.
- **Use Checklists**: Add checklists to cards to break down tasks into smaller steps. Check off items as they are completed.
- **Attach Files**: Attach relevant documents, images, or links to cards for easy access and reference.
- **Comment and Collaborate**: Use the comment feature to communicate with team members directly on cards. Tag team members to notify them of updates or questions.
- **Track Progress**: Move cards across lists as tasks progress from "To Do" to "In Progress" and finally to "Completed."

Enhancing Team Collaboration

Effective collaboration is essential for project success. Here are some tips for enhancing team collaboration:

1. **Foster a Collaborative Culture**: Encourage open communication, mutual respect, and teamwork. Create an environment where team members feel comfortable sharing ideas and feedback.
2. **Use Collaboration Tools**: Utilize tools like Slack, Microsoft Teams, and Google Workspace to facilitate communication and collaboration. These tools support real-time messaging, file sharing, and document collaboration.
3. **Hold Regular Team Meetings**: Schedule regular meetings to discuss progress, address challenges, and plan next steps. Use these meetings to foster collaboration and ensure everyone is aligned.
4. **Encourage Cross-Functional Collaboration**: Promote collaboration between different departments or teams to

leverage diverse perspectives and expertise. Cross-functional collaboration can lead to more innovative solutions.

5. **Set Clear Expectations**: Clearly define roles, responsibilities, and expectations for team members. Ensure that everyone understands their contributions and how they fit into the overall project.

6. **Recognize and Reward Collaboration**: Acknowledge and reward team members who demonstrate strong collaboration skills. Recognition reinforces positive behaviour and motivates others to collaborate effectively.

7. **Provide Opportunities for Social Interaction**: Organize team-building activities and social events to strengthen relationships and build trust among team members. Strong personal connections enhance collaboration.

Practical Tips for Managing Remote Teams

Managing remote teams presents unique challenges, but with the right strategies, you can ensure effective collaboration and productivity. Here are some tips for managing remote teams:

1. **Set Clear Communication Guidelines**: Establish clear guidelines for communication, including preferred channels, response times, and meeting schedules. Consistent communication helps keep remote teams aligned.

2. **Use Video Conferencing**: Use video conferencing tools like Zoom or Microsoft Teams for meetings. Video calls help build stronger connections and improve communication compared to audio-only calls.

3. **Foster a Sense of Community**: Create opportunities for remote team members to connect and socialize. Use

virtual team-building activities and encourage informal communication.

4. **Provide the Right Tools**: Ensure that remote team members have access to the necessary tools and resources, such as project management software, communication platforms, and file-sharing solutions.

5. **Set Clear Goals and Expectations**: Define clear goals, deadlines, and performance expectations for remote team members. Regularly review progress and provide feedback.

6. **Encourage Flexibility**: Recognize that remote team members may have different work schedules and environments. Allow flexibility in work hours while ensuring that deadlines and commitments are met.

7. **Monitor Well-Being**: Pay attention to the well-being of remote team members. Check in regularly to discuss any challenges they may be facing and offer support as needed.

By implementing these tips and tricks, you can enhance your project management skills, improve organization, and boost team collaboration and productivity. Utilizing project management tools, effective time management techniques, and fostering a collaborative culture are key to successful project outcomes. In the next chapter, we will explore common challenges in project management and how to overcome them, providing strategies and solutions to address various obstacles that may arise.

Chapter 9: Common Challenges and How to Overcome Them

Project management is fraught with challenges that can arise at any stage of the project lifecycle. Being able to identify, address, and overcome these challenges is crucial for the success of any project. In this chapter, we will explore common challenges in project management and provide strategies and solutions to address them.

Challenge 1: Scope Creep

Scope creep occurs when additional features or tasks are added to a project without corresponding adjustments to time, budget, or resources. This can lead to project delays, cost overruns, and compromised quality.

Strategies to Overcome Scope Creep:

1. **Clearly Define Scope**: Establish a detailed project scope at the beginning, including specific deliverables and exclusions. Document this in a scope statement and get stakeholder approval.
2. **Implement Change Control Processes**: Use a formal change control process to evaluate and approve changes to the project scope. Any changes should be documented, and their impact on time, budget, and resources should be assessed.
3. **Communicate Scope Boundaries**: Regularly communicate the project scope and any approved changes to all stakeholders and team members. Ensure everyone

understands what is included and excluded from the project.

4. **Monitor and Control Scope**: Continuously monitor the project to identify any deviations from the original scope. Use project management tools to track scope changes and their impact.

5. **Engage Stakeholders**: Involve stakeholders in scope discussions and decision-making. Ensure they understand the implications of scope changes and are aligned with the project's goals.

Challenge 2: Poor Communication

Effective communication is critical to project success. Poor communication can lead to misunderstandings, misaligned expectations, and missed deadlines.

Strategies to Overcome Poor Communication:

1. **Develop a Communication Plan**: Create a detailed communication plan that outlines how, when, and what information will be communicated to stakeholders and team members. Include communication methods, frequency, and responsible parties.

2. **Use Communication Tools**: Utilize communication tools like Slack, Microsoft Teams, or Zoom to facilitate real-time communication and collaboration. These tools support various communication methods, such as messaging, video calls, and file sharing.

3. **Schedule Regular Meetings**: Hold regular team meetings to discuss progress, address issues, and plan next steps. Use these meetings to ensure everyone is aligned and informed.

4. **Encourage Open Communication**: Foster a culture of open communication where team members feel comfortable sharing ideas, asking questions, and providing feedback. Encourage active listening and constructive dialogue.
5. **Provide Clear Instructions**: Ensure that all instructions and expectations are clearly communicated. Use written documentation and visual aids to enhance understanding and reduce the risk of misinterpretation.

Challenge 3: Inadequate Risk Management

Risks are inherent in any project, and inadequate risk management can lead to unexpected issues and project failure.

Strategies to Overcome Inadequate Risk Management:

1. **Identify Risks Early**: Conduct a thorough risk assessment at the beginning of the project to identify potential risks. Use brainstorming sessions, checklists, and risk assessment tools to identify risks.
2. **Develop a Risk Management Plan**: Create a risk management plan that outlines how risks will be identified, assessed, and mitigated. Include strategies for addressing high-priority risks.
3. **Monitor Risks Continuously**: Continuously monitor risks throughout the project lifecycle. Use risk registers to track identified risks, their status, and mitigation efforts.
4. **Implement Mitigation Strategies**: Develop and implement mitigation strategies for identified risks. Assign responsibility for managing each risk and ensure that mitigation efforts are documented and monitored.
5. **Conduct Regular Risk Reviews**: Schedule regular risk reviews to assess the effectiveness of mitigation strategies

and identify any new risks. Use these reviews to update the risk management plan as needed.

Challenge 4: Resource Constraints

Resource constraints, such as limited budget, time, or personnel, can impact the project's ability to meet its objectives.

Strategies to Overcome Resource Constraints:

1. **Accurate Resource Planning**: Conduct thorough resource planning at the beginning of the project to identify the resources needed. Use resource estimation techniques to ensure accuracy.
2. **Prioritize Tasks**: Prioritize tasks based on their importance and impact on the project. Allocate resources to high-priority tasks first to ensure critical activities are completed.
3. **Optimize Resource Utilization**: Use resource management tools to optimize resource utilization. Track resource allocation and adjust as needed to avoid overloading or underutilizing team members.
4. **Negotiate for Additional Resources**: If resource constraints become a significant issue, negotiate with stakeholders for additional resources. Provide evidence of the need and potential impact on the project.
5. **Implement Time Management Techniques**: Use time management techniques, such as time blocking and the Pomodoro Technique, to enhance productivity and make the most of available time.

Challenge 5: Stakeholder Management

Managing stakeholder expectations and involvement can be challenging, especially when dealing with multiple stakeholders with varying interests.

Strategies to Overcome Stakeholder Management Issues:

1. **Identify Stakeholders Early**: Identify all relevant stakeholders at the beginning of the project. Understand their interests, expectations, and influence on the project.
2. **Develop a Stakeholder Engagement Plan**: Create a stakeholder engagement plan that outlines how stakeholders will be involved and communicated with throughout the project. Include strategies for managing different types of stakeholders.
3. **Maintain Regular Communication**: Keep stakeholders informed with regular updates on the project's progress. Use status reports, meetings, and presentations to communicate key information.
4. **Manage Expectations**: Set realistic expectations with stakeholders from the beginning. Clearly communicate the project's scope, timeline, and potential challenges.
5. **Address Stakeholder Concerns**: Actively listen to stakeholder concerns and address them promptly. Provide clear explanations and solutions to build trust and maintain positive relationships.

Challenge 6: Poor Team Collaboration

Lack of collaboration among team members can lead to inefficiencies, misunderstandings, and decreased productivity.

Strategies to Overcome Poor Team Collaboration:

1. **Foster a Collaborative Culture**: Create a culture that values collaboration and teamwork. Encourage team members to share ideas, provide feedback, and support each other.
2. **Use Collaboration Tools**: Utilize collaboration tools like Microsoft Teams, Trello, or Asana to facilitate communication and coordination among team members. These tools support real-time updates and task management.
3. **Define Roles and Responsibilities**: Clearly define the roles and responsibilities of each team member. Ensure everyone understands their tasks and how they contribute to the project's success.
4. **Schedule Regular Team Meetings**: Hold regular team meetings to discuss progress, address challenges, and plan next steps. Use these meetings to ensure everyone is aligned and informed.
5. **Encourage Social Interaction**: Organize team-building activities and social events to strengthen relationships and build trust among team members. Strong personal connections enhance collaboration.

Challenge 7: Unrealistic Deadlines

Unrealistic deadlines can lead to stress, decreased quality, and project failure.

Strategies to Overcome Unrealistic Deadlines:

1. **Set Realistic Schedules**: Use accurate estimation techniques to set realistic project schedules. Consider factors such as task complexity, resource availability, and potential risks.

2. **Communicate Constraints**: Clearly communicate any constraints or limitations to stakeholders. Ensure they understand the impact of unrealistic deadlines on the project's quality and success.
3. **Negotiate Deadlines**: Negotiate deadlines with stakeholders based on realistic estimates. Provide evidence and rationale for the proposed timeline.
4. **Prioritize Tasks**: Focus on high-priority tasks that are critical to the project's success. Allocate resources to these tasks first to ensure they are completed on time.
5. **Monitor Progress**: Continuously monitor progress and adjust the schedule as needed. Use project management tools to track deadlines and identify any potential delays early.

Challenge 8: Inadequate Planning

Inadequate planning can lead to missed deadlines, cost overruns, and project failure.

Strategies to Overcome Inadequate Planning:

1. **Thorough Initial Planning**: Invest time in thorough initial planning to develop a detailed project plan. Include key elements such as scope, schedule, budget, resources, and risk management.
2. **Involve Stakeholders in Planning**: Involve stakeholders in the planning process to ensure their expectations are considered and to gain their support. Use their input to develop a comprehensive plan.
3. **Use Planning Tools**: Utilize project management tools like Gantt charts, work breakdown structures (WBS), and critical path method (CPM) to create detailed and accurate project plans.

4. **Regularly Review and Update Plans**: Continuously review and update the project plan based on new information and changing circumstances. Schedule regular review sessions to ensure the plan remains relevant and effective.
5. **Document Assumptions and Constraints**: Clearly document any assumptions and constraints that impact the project plan. Use this documentation to manage expectations and address any potential issues.

By understanding and addressing these common challenges, you can enhance your project management skills and improve the likelihood of project success. Implementing strategies for managing scope creep, communication, risk, resources, stakeholders, collaboration, deadlines, and planning will help you navigate obstacles and achieve your project objectives. In the next chapter, we will explore the role of habits in effective time management and provide practical tips for developing positive habits that support productivity and project success.

Chapter 10: The Role of Habits in Effective Time Management

Effective time management is not only about using the right tools and techniques but also about cultivating the right habits. Habits are powerful because they shape our daily actions and routines, allowing us to manage our time more efficiently and achieve our goals more consistently. In this chapter, we will explore the role of habits in effective time management, the science behind habit formation, and practical tips for developing positive habits that support productivity and project success.

Understanding Habits

Habits are automatic behaviours that are triggered by specific cues and reinforced through repetition. They can be positive, such as exercising regularly, or negative, such as procrastinating. Understanding how habits work can help you develop habits that enhance your productivity and time management skills.

Components of a Habit:

1. **Cue**: The trigger that initiates the habit. This could be a specific time of day, an emotional state, or an environmental cue.
2. **Routine**: The behaviour or action that follows the cue. This is the habit itself.
3. **Reward**: The positive reinforcement that follows the routine, making the habit more likely to be repeated in the future.

Example of a Habit Loop:

- **Cue**: Seeing your workout clothes laid out in the morning.
- **Routine**: Going for a run.
- **Reward**: Feeling energized and accomplished after the run.

The Science Behind Habit Formation

Understanding the science behind habit formation can help you intentionally develop habits that support your time management goals. According to research, it takes an average of 66 days to form a new habit, although this can vary depending on the complexity of the habit and individual differences.

Key Principles of Habit Formation:

1. **Start Small**: Begin with small, manageable changes that are easy to incorporate into your routine. Gradually build up to more significant changes.
2. **Be Consistent**: Consistency is key to forming new habits. Aim to perform the habit at the same time and in the same context every day.
3. **Use Positive Reinforcement**: Reinforce the habit with positive rewards. This could be a sense of accomplishment, a treat, or any other reward that motivates you.
4. **Track Progress**: Keep track of your progress to stay motivated and accountable. Use habit trackers, journals, or apps to monitor your consistency.
5. **Stay Patient**: Forming new habits takes time and effort. Be patient with yourself and stay committed, even if you encounter setbacks.

Developing Positive Habits for Time Management

Here are some practical tips for developing positive habits that support effective time management:

1. **Prioritize Tasks with a Daily To-Do List**: Make it a habit to create a daily to-do list every morning. Prioritize tasks based on their importance and urgency. Use tools like the Eisenhower Matrix to categorize tasks and focus on high-priority activities.

2. **Set Clear Goals**: Develop the habit of setting clear, achievable goals. Use the SMART criteria (Specific, Measurable, Achievable, Relevant, Time-bound) to define your goals and track your progress.

3. **Use Time Blocks**: Incorporate time blocking into your daily routine. Allocate specific blocks of time for different tasks and activities. This helps you stay focused and ensures that you dedicate sufficient time to important tasks.

4. **Limit Distractions**: Develop habits that minimize distractions. For example, set specific times to check emails and messages, and create a dedicated workspace free from interruptions.

5. **Take Regular Breaks**: Make it a habit to take regular breaks throughout the day. Use techniques like the Pomodoro Technique to work in focused intervals, followed by short breaks to rest and recharge.

6. **Reflect and Review**: At the end of each day, take a few minutes to reflect on your accomplishments and areas for improvement. Review your to-do list, evaluate your progress, and plan for the next day.

7. **Practice Mindfulness**: Incorporate mindfulness practices into your routine to enhance focus and reduce stress. This could include meditation, deep breathing exercises, or simply taking a few moments to be present and mindful.

Example of a Daily Routine with Positive Time Management Habits:

Time	Activity	Habit Focus
7:00 AM	Morning workout	Start the day with energy
8:00 AM	Create daily to-do list	Prioritize tasks
8:30 AM	Focused work (Time block 1)	Limit distractions
10:30 AM	Short break	Take regular breaks
10:45 AM	Focused work (Time block 2)	Use time blocks
12:45 PM	Lunch break	Recharge
1:30 PM	Check emails and messages	Manage distractions
2:00 PM	Focused work (Time block 3)	Maintain focus
4:00 PM	Short break	Take regular breaks
4:15 PM	Review progress and plan for next day	Reflect and review
5:00 PM	End workday	Maintain work-life balance

Overcoming Challenges in Habit Formation

Forming new habits can be challenging, and it's common to encounter obstacles along the way. Here are some strategies to overcome common challenges:

1. **Lack of Motivation**: Identify your "why" – the underlying reason for wanting to develop the habit. Keeping your motivation in mind can help you stay committed.

2. **Procrastination**: Break tasks into smaller, manageable steps. Start with the smallest step to build momentum and reduce the tendency to procrastinate.
3. **Inconsistency**: Set reminders and use habit-tracking tools to maintain consistency. Celebrate small wins to reinforce the habit and stay motivated.
4. **Negative Self-Talk**: Replace negative self-talk with positive affirmations. Focus on your progress and potential rather than setbacks.
5. **Environmental Triggers**: Modify your environment to support your new habits. Remove triggers that lead to negative habits and create cues that prompt positive behaviours.

Example of Using Habit-Tracking Tools:

- **Habit Tracker Apps**: Use apps like Habitica, Streaks, or HabitBull to track your habits, set reminders, and visualize your progress.
- **Bullet Journal**: Maintain a bullet journal to record your daily habits, track progress, and reflect on your achievements.
- **Wall Calendar**: Use a wall calendar to mark off days when you successfully complete your habit. Seeing a visual representation of your consistency can be motivating.

Integrating Habits into Project Management

Incorporating positive habits into your project management practices can enhance your efficiency and effectiveness. Here are some ways to integrate habits into your project management routine:

1. **Daily Stand-Up Meetings**: Develop the habit of holding daily stand-up meetings with your project team. These brief meetings provide an opportunity to discuss progress, address challenges, and align on priorities.
2. **Weekly Reviews**: Schedule weekly reviews to evaluate the project's progress, assess risks, and make necessary adjustments. Use these reviews to celebrate successes and identify areas for improvement.
3. **Task Delegation**: Make it a habit to delegate tasks effectively. Clearly define responsibilities, set expectations, and provide support to team members.
4. **Continuous Learning**: Cultivate the habit of continuous learning. Stay updated on project management best practices, tools, and techniques. Encourage your team to participate in training and development opportunities.
5. **Risk Management**: Regularly review and update your risk management plan. Develop the habit of proactively identifying and mitigating risks to minimize their impact on the project.

Example of Integrating Habits into Project Management:

- **Daily Stand-Up Meetings**: Hold a 15-minute stand-up meeting every morning to discuss what was accomplished yesterday, what is planned for today, and any roadblocks.
- **Weekly Reviews**: Schedule a one-hour weekly review meeting every Friday to assess the project's progress, review milestones, and adjust plans as needed.
- **Task Delegation**: Use a project management tool to assign tasks to team members, set deadlines, and track progress. Regularly check in to provide support and address any issues.

- **Continuous Learning**: Allocate time for team members to attend webinars, workshops, or training sessions. Share key takeaways and best practices with the team.
- **Risk Management**: Review the risk register during weekly reviews and update mitigation strategies. Encourage team members to identify new risks and discuss potential impacts.

By developing positive habits and integrating them into your daily routine and project management practices, you can enhance your productivity, manage your time more effectively, and achieve your goals. Understanding the science behind habit formation, staying consistent, and using tools to track progress are key to building habits that support success. In the next chapter, we will provide closing remarks and summarize the key takeaways from this book, reinforcing the importance of effective time management and project management skills.

Chapter 11: Closing Remarks

Congratulations on reaching the end of "Teach Your Granny Project Management." By now, you have gained valuable insights and practical knowledge to manage projects effectively. Whether you're organizing a family event, launching a new product, or leading a complex project at work, the principles and techniques discussed in this book will help you achieve your goals with confidence.

Key Takeaways

Let's recap some of the key takeaways from each chapter to reinforce what you've learned and highlight the essential elements of successful project management.

Chapter 1: Understanding Project Management

- A project is a temporary endeavour with a unique goal, defined scope, and specific deliverables.
- Project management involves planning, organizing, leading, and controlling resources to achieve project objectives.
- The project lifecycle includes initiation, planning, execution, monitoring and controlling, and closing.

Chapter 2: Defining Your Project

- Clearly define project objectives and goals using the SMART criteria.
- Establish a well-defined project scope to set boundaries and manage expectations.

- Identify and analyse stakeholders to understand their needs and influence.
- Create a project charter to formally authorize the project and provide a high-level overview.

Chapter 3: Planning Your Project

- Develop a comprehensive project plan that includes objectives, scope, work breakdown structure (WBS), schedule, budget, and risk management.
- Use tools like Gantt charts and resource plans to visualize and manage project tasks and timelines.
- Allocate resources effectively and monitor their usage throughout the project.

Chapter 4: Organizing Your Project

- Build a strong project team by identifying required skills, selecting team members, and defining roles and responsibilities.
- Establish clear communication channels and protocols to ensure effective collaboration.
- Use project management tools to keep track of tasks, deadlines, and progress.

Chapter 5: Leading Your Project Team

- Balance leadership and management skills to inspire, motivate, and guide your team.
- Set clear goals and expectations, provide recognition and rewards, and create a positive work environment.
- Practice effective communication strategies and address conflicts promptly.

Chapter 6: Controlling and Monitoring Your Project

- Track project progress using key performance indicators (KPIs) and project management tools.
- Implement change control processes to manage changes to the project scope, schedule, and budget.
- Maintain quality through regular inspections, testing, and quality assurance activities.

Chapter 7: Closing Your Project

- Finalize deliverables, obtain stakeholder approval, and conduct a thorough project review.
- Document lessons learned and share best practices with the team and stakeholders.
- Celebrate project success and plan for future projects.

Chapter 8: Tips and Tricks for Successful Project Management

- Stay organized with tools like Trello, Asana, and Microsoft Project.
- Manage time effectively using techniques like the Pomodoro Technique, time blocking, and SMART goals.
- Foster collaboration and communication within the team and leverage tools to enhance productivity.

Chapter 9: Common Challenges and How to Overcome Them

- Address common project management challenges such as scope creep, poor communication, inadequate risk management, and resource constraints.
- Implement strategies to manage stakeholder expectations, improve team collaboration, and set realistic deadlines.

Chapter 10: The Role of Habits in Effective Time Management

- Develop positive habits that support effective time management and productivity.
- Understand the science behind habit formation and use habit-tracking tools to stay consistent.
- Integrate habits into your project management routine to enhance efficiency and effectiveness.

Looking Ahead

Effective project management is a valuable skill that can be applied to various aspects of life and work. By mastering the principles and techniques outlined in this book, you can tackle projects with confidence, achieve your goals, and contribute to the success of your team and organization.

Remember that project management is an ongoing learning process. Continuously seek opportunities to improve your skills, stay updated on best practices, and adapt to new challenges. Embrace a growth mindset and be open to feedback and learning from your experiences.

Final Words

Thank you for embarking on this journey to learn about project management. I hope that the insights and strategies shared in this book have equipped you with the tools you need to succeed. Whether you're a seasoned project manager or new to the field, the principles of effective project management are universal and can help you achieve remarkable results.

Stay organized, communicate effectively, and lead with confidence. As you apply what you've learned, you'll find that managing projects becomes more intuitive and rewarding. Here's to your continued success in all your project management endeavours.

Warmest regards,

Andy